The Big Bang Theory Cookbook

Not So Gastronomically Redundant
Cookbook

Table of Contents

Introduction 4

Chapter 1: Drinks and Starters 6

    1. Steamed Dumpling.................7

    2. Hobbit Pancakes 9

    3. Hot Chocolate with Peppermint Schnapps.................. 11

    4. Chips and Salsa 13

    5. Cuba Libre 15

Chapter 2: Main Course 17

    6. Sheldon's Spaghetti.................. 18

    7. Beer Battered Fish.................. 20

    8.Barbeque Bacon Cheeseburger 22

    9. Burrito Grand 24

    10. Egg Rolls.................. 26

    11. Kung Pao Chicken 29

    12. Kadhai Paneer 32

    13. Tangerine Chicken 35

    14. Quesadilla with Soy sauce 38

    15. Shrimp Caesar Salad.................. 41

    16.Chicken Satay.................. 43

    17. Beef Brisket.................. 46

    18. Mee Krob 48

    19. Giacomo's Pizza! 50

20. Beef with Broccoli 52

21. Peach Cobbler Chicken 54

22. Cashew Chicken 56

23. Vegetable Lo Mein 58

24. Shrimp in Mobster sauce.. 60

25. General Tso's Chicken 63

Chapter 3: Desserts.. 66

26. Raj's Tapioca Pudding.. 67

27. Sheldon's Birthday Cake.. 69

28. Nutty Muffins.. 72

29. Memaw's Christmas Cookies 74

30. Ice Cream with Kalua... 76

Conclusion 78

Introduction

Are you on the lookout for meal ideas for a Big Bang Theory themed party? Do you wish to recreate delicacies from the Cheesecake Factory? Are you searching for the perfect finger food to gorge on while going through hours of reruns? You have come to the right place!

This cookbook is designed to capture the essence of The Big Bang Theory and throw light on some of its best moments. The show might have come to an end, after 12 seasons of fun and laughter, but your love for it does not have to! Come fall in love with it once again and start your Big Bang Theory-culinary journey!

At the end of this cookbook, you are left with 30 starter, entrée and dessert recipes that are easy to make and delicious to taste. Seasoned with trivia, these recipes are sure to be a hit amongst friends and family. Prepare for hours of fun trying out these dishes and engaging in endless conversations about your favorite show!

Rock, Paper, Scissors, Spock, Lizard, let's go!

Chapter 1: Drinks and Starters

1. Steamed Dumpling

Sheldon orders steamed dumplings as part of the meal. He thinks its perfect since the plate contains 4 pieces and each of them gets one.

Serving size: 4-6

Cooking time: 30 minutes

Ingredients:

- ½ lb pork, minced
- 10 small prawns, cleaned
- 1 celery stalk, chopped

- 1 teaspoon ginger, chopped
- ½ tablespoon vinegar
- 1 teaspoon soy sauce
- 1 teaspoon sesame oil
- Salt and pepper to taste
- 1 pack wonton wrappers

Instructions:

1. Add the pork mince, prawns, celery, sesame oil and ginger to a bowl along with salt and pepper and mix well.

2. Take a tablespoonful of the mix and place it in the center of a wonton wrapper.

3. Apply a little water to the edges and fold the dumplings.

4. Place them inside a bamboo steamer and steam for 10 minutes.

5. Mix the soy sauce and vinegar together.

6. Serve warm with soya sauce dip.

2. Hobbit Pancakes

The gang often has hobbit shaped pancakes for breakfast and use coconut shavings for feet hair.

Serving size: 6-8

Cooking time: 20 minutes

Ingredients:

- 1 ¾ cup flour
- ½ tablespoon lemon juice
- 2 tablespoons sugar
- 1 ¼ cup whole milk
- 1 egg
- 4 tablespoons butter

- 4 teaspoons baking powder
- Pinch of salt
- Coconut shavings

Instructions:

1. Add flour, salt, sugar and baking powder to a bowl and mix.

2. Add in milk, butter and egg and fold until smooth.

3. Place a hobbit shaped stencil over hot griddle and pour a ladleful of the mixture in the center.

4. Brown the pancake on both sides.

5. Serve with a sprinkling of coconut shavings on the feet.

3. Hot Chocolate with Peppermint Schnapps

Hot chocolate is a prominent feature in the series. Sheldon prefers regular hot chocolate, with real cocoa, on game night. The others settle for an adult version. Here is the recipe for it.

Serving size: 5

Cooking time: 10 minutes

Ingredients:

- 4 cups milk
- 10 ounces peppermint schnapps
- 5 ounces semi-sweet chocolate

- Whipped cream

Instructions:

1. Add milk to a saucepan and heat on low flame.

2. Toss in the chocolate and whisk it until well combined.

3. Pour into a cup and mix in peppermint schnapps.

4. Add whipped cream on top and serve.

4. Chips and Salsa

Potato chips and salsa are a common accompaniment that Raj orders at the Cheesecake Factory.

Serving size: 2

Cooking time: 30 minutes

Ingredients:

For chips

- 5 potatoes
- Oil to drizzle
- Salt and pepper to taste

For salsa

- 4 tomatoes
- 1 small onion
- 1 small chili
- ½ cup cilantro leaves, chopped
- Salt and pepper to taste

Instructions:

1. Preheat oven to 400 Fahrenheit.

2. Wash, peel and cut the potatoes into 1 cm pieces.

3. Add them to a bowl along with the oil, salt and pepper and arrange on a lined baking tray.

4. Bake for 25 to 30 minutes or until crispy.

5. To make the salsa, add the onion, chili, cilantro leaves and tomatoes to a bowl and mix with salt and pepper.

6. Cover and rest for an hour.

7. Serve with hot chips.

5. Cuba Libre

Before taking up the bar tending role at the Cheesecake Factory, Penny asks the boys to help her practice her skills. Sheldon says he wants a virgin Cuba Libre, meaning just a coke, and asks it to be diet. You, however, do not have to settle for a virgin libre and go for this zingy, zesty cocktail!

Serving size: 1

Cooking time: 5 minutes

Ingredients:

- 1 small lime
- 2 ounces rum
- 4 ounces coke
- Ice cubes

Instructions:

1. Juice the lime and add to a glass.

2. Zest its skin and mix it in.

3. Pour in the rum and coke and stir.

4. Serve with a few ice cubes.

Chapter 2: Main Course

6. Sheldon's Spaghetti

Sheldon loves his spaghetti with cut up pieces of hot dog. His mom often made it when he was a child. Amy makes it for him during a dinner date to ignite affectionate feelings.

Serving size: 6

Cooking time: 1 hour

Ingredients:

- 2 hot dogs
- 1 pack spaghetti
- 1 tablespoon olive oil
- 1 bell pepper, chopped

- 1 cup tomato puree
- 1 teaspoon garlic, chopped
- 1 teaspoon basil leaves
- 1 teaspoon oregano leaves
- 1 teaspoon sugar
- Salt and pepper to taste

Instructions:

1. Boil water in a pot and add the spaghetti and cook till soft.

2. Add oil to a pan and toss in the onions.

3. Add garlic mince and sauté until brown.

4. Add the bell peppers and throw in the oregano and basil leaves.

5. Season with salt and pepper and mix in cut up hot dogs.

6. Pour in the tomato puree and sugar and cook on low flame for 15 minutes.

7. Add in cooked spaghetti and cook for 10 minutes.

8. Serve hot.

7. Beer Battered Fish

Raj loves a generous helping of beer battered fish that he enjoys with tartar sauce. You too will fall in love with it once you taste this recipe!

Serving size: 4

Cooking time: 30 minutes

Ingredients:

- 4 ounces codfish fillet
- 1 cup flour
- 1 tablespoon garlic, chopped

- 1 tablespoon paprika
- 1 egg
- Salt and pepper to taste
- 1 bottle beer
- Oil for frying

Instructions:

1. Add oil to a pan or fryer and heat to 365 Fahrenheit.

2. Clean the fish fillet and place it on a plate.

3. Sprinkle with salt and pepper.

4. Add the garlic, flour, paprika, salt and pepper to a bowl and beat in the egg.

5. Pour in the beer and mix until well combined.

6. Dip in the seasoned cod and place it in the oil.

7. Fry for 4 to 5 minutes or until brown on both sides.

8. Serve hot with chips and salsa.

8.Barbeque Bacon Cheeseburger

Sheldon loves digging into barbeque bacon cheeseburgers and why not? It is easily one of the tastiest comfort foods out there. Don't believe me? Try it for yourself!

Serving size: 6

Cooking time: 35 minutes

Ingredients:

- 12 bacon slices
- 1 lb beef, minced
- 1 large onion
- 1 cup barbeque sauce
- 1 tablespoon burger seasoning

- 4 cheese slices
- 4 burger buns, cut in half
- 4 lettuce leaves

Instructions:

1. Add the bacon to a pan and cook till crispy.

2. Remove and set aside.

3. Place the buns over the pan and brown on the inner sides.

4. Add the beef mince, salt and pepper and make patties.

5. Place them over the pan and brown on all sides.

6. Place a lettuce leaf on one side of the bun.

7. Place a patty over the lettuce leaf and drizzle the barbeque sauce.

8. Cut the onion into circles and place over the patties.

9. Place a couple of bacon slices over it.

10. Cover with the other half and serve hot.

9. Burrito Grand

Leonard likes his burritos without cheese and sour cream but you don't have to! This recipe for a simple yet delicious burrito is perfect for dinner parties.

Serving size: 6

Cooking time: 50 minutes

Ingredients:

- 1 cup refried beans
- 1 cup corn
- 1 lb beef, minced

- 2 ounces seasoning
- 2 cups rice, cooked
- 2 tablespoons sour cream
- 2 tablespoons salsa
- 5 tortillas
- ½ cup cheddar cheese
- Salt and pepper to taste

Instructions:

1. Preheat the oven to 375 Fahrenheit.

2. Add oil to a pan and cook the beef.

3. Sprinkle salt, pepper and taco seasoning.

4. To make a burrito, place a tortilla on a plate and add 4 tablespoons of beans in the middle.

5. Place 6 tablespoons of rice over it and pat down slightly.

6. Add 5 tablespoons of the beef mixture over it followed by 1 tablespoon corn and 5 tablespoons cheese.

7. Wrap it up and bake for 25 minutes.

8. Serve with a drizzle of salsa and sour cream on top.

10. Egg Rolls

Sheldon finds it annoying when Penny dips her egg rolls twice using her hands. She then switches over to chopsticks in future episodes.

Serving size: 10

Cooking time: 30 minutes

Ingredients:

- 1 lb pork, minced
- ½ inch ginger, minced
- 1 teaspoon garlic, minced
- 1 tablespoon soy sauce
- 1 small onion, chopped
- ½ tablespoon sesame oil
- 2 cups coleslaw
- 10 egg roll wrappers
- Salt and pepper to taste
- 1 egg

Instructions:

1. Add oil to a pan along with pork, pepper and salt and cook until it browns.

2. Add in garlic and ginger along with soy sauce and sesame oil and mix.

3. Add in the coleslaw and cook for 2 minutes.

4. Place the egg wrapper on a plate and add 2 tablespoons of the filling in the center of the wrapper and roll.

5. Apply a little beaten egg to the edges to help them stick.

6. Heat oil in a pan or fryer.

7. Fry for 6 minutes or until brown and crispy.

11. Kung Pao Chicken

Raj goes for Kung Pao Chicken on Chinese takeout nights. A simple yet delicious dish, Kung Pao Chicken is perfect for Chinese dinners.

Serving size: 4

Cooking time: 40 minutes

Ingredients:

- 1 teaspoon vinegar
- 2 teaspoons corn starch

- ½ tablespoon soy sauce
- 1 lb chicken breast
- For sauce
- 1 teaspoon soy sauce
- ½ teaspoon sesame oil
- 1 teaspoon sugar
- 1 tablespoon balsamic vinegar
- 1 teaspoon Schezuan pepper
- 1 tablespoon garlic, chopped
- ½ inch ginger, minced
- 5 tablespoon roasted peanuts
- 1 teaspoon peanut oil
- 10-12 spring onions, chopped
- Salt to taste

Instructions:

1. Add soy sauce, vinegar and corn starch to a bowl along with pieces of chicken breast and mix.

2. Set aside for 30 minutes.

3. To make the sauce, add the soy sauce, sesame oil, sugar, balsamic vinegar, Schezuan pepper, salt, garlic and ginger and mix until well combined.

4. Heat a pan or a wok and the peanut oil and fry the chicken for 4 minutes.

5. Toss in the garlic and ginger and stir fry for 2 minutes.

6. Pour in the sauce and cook for a minute.

7. Serve with chopped spring onions on top.

12. Kadhai Paneer

Kadhai Paneer is a delicious Indian curry made with cottage cheese and served with rice or roti. Raj, however, loathes the dish. But don't worry, unlike him, you will fall in love with this rich, saucy dish and lick every last drop from your plate!

Serving size: 4

Cooking time: 30 minutes

Ingredients:

- 1 pack paneer cubes
- 1 tablespoon vegetable oil

- ½ tablespoon butter
- 1 onion, cut into squares
- 1 green bell pepper, cut into squares
- 1 chilli, chopped
- ½ inch ginger, minced
- 2 teaspoons garlic, minced
- 3 tomatoes, chopped
- 1 teaspoon Indian curry powder
- 1 teaspoon red chili powder
- 1 teaspoon dried Kasuri Methi leaves (fenugreek leaves)
- 5 ounces water
- 1 tablespoon cream
- Salt to taste
- Coriander leaves, chopped

Instructions:

1. Add the oil and butter to a pan and toss in the paneer cubes, onion and bell pepper.

2. Brown them on all sides and remove.

3. Add the ginger and garlic along with tomatoes and cook until they turn soft.

4. Add in the chilies, curry powder, chili powder, salt and water and bring to a boil.

5. Add in the browned paneer, onion and bell peppers and cook until soft.

6. Add in the fenugreek leaves and finish with a dollop of fresh cream on top.

7. Serve with rice or roti and a sprinkling of fresh coriander leaves on top.

13. Tangerine Chicken

Schezuan Palace is a frequently featured restaurant in the series. Sheldon usually orders Tangerine chicken for himself during the first few seasons, before the restaurant closes down, without his knowledge.

Serving size: 4

Cooking time: 45 minutes (5 hours marinate)

Ingredients:

- 5 tablespoons soy sauce
- 5 tablespoons honey

- 2 teaspoons garlic, minced
- 2 teaspoons ginger, minced
- 2 teaspoons sesame oil
- 1 teaspoon cinnamon powder
- 3 lb chicken breast
- 3 tangerines
- Salt and pepper to taste

Instructions:

1. Peel the skin of the tangerines and cut them finely.

2. Extract 1 cup of juice and add to a bowl along with the peel.

3. Add in soy sauce, garlic, ginger, oil, honey and cinnamon and mix until well combined.

4. Add in the chicken breasts, salt and pepper and coat them completely.

5. Refrigerate for 5 to 6 hours.

6. Preheat oven to 375 Fahrenheit.

7. Place the chicken on a tray and pour the sauce on top.

8. Bake for 40 minutes or until the chicken is tender.

9. Serve hot.

14. Quesadilla with Soy sauce

Leonard is lactose intolerant and avoids dairy. He orders for himself quesadillas with soy sauce at the Cheesecake Factory. Here is a delicious version of it.

Serving size: 4

Cooking time: 45 minutes

Ingredients:

- 5 tablespoons soy sauce
- 1 teaspoon garlic, chopped
- ½ teaspoon sesame oil
- 1 teaspoon olive oil
- 1 tablespoon sugar
- 1 tablespoon corn starch
- ½ lb chicken breast
- 1 cup broccoli florets
- 5 tortilla
- 5 tablespoons salsa
- 2 ounces cheddar cheese

Instructions:

1. Add the garlic to a bowl along with the oil, soy sauce, water, sugar and corn starch and whisk until combined.

2. Boil water in a pot and toss in the broccoli.

3. Cook for 4 minutes and take them out.

4. Add olive oil to a skillet and brown the chicken.

5. Add the broccoli in along with the soy sauce mixture and stir together.

6. Place the tortilla on a plate and add 5 tablespoons of the chicken mixture in the center.

7. Spoon 3 tablespoons of salsa over it.

8. Add grated cheese on top and close the tortilla.

9. Place in a preheated 375 oven for 10 minutes.

10. Cut and serve.

15. Shrimp Caesar Salad

Howard orders himself Shrimp Caesar Salad without almonds on Jewish High Holidays. Easy to make, this salad is a filling lunch option.

Serving size: 4

Cooking time: 25 minutes

Ingredients:

- 1 lemon
- 1 teaspoon mustard
- 5 tablespoons mayonnaise

- 1 teaspoon tabasco sauce
- 1 anchovy, chopped
- 1 teaspoon garlic, minced
- 5 teaspoons olive oil
- 1 lb shrimp, cleaned
- Salt and pepper to taste

Instructions:

1. Juice the lemon and grate its rind.

2. Add to a bowl along with mustard, tabasco, garlic, anchovy, 1 tablespoon oil, salt, pepper and mayonnaise and mix.

3. Heat grill and brush oil.

4. Add in the shrimp and cook till grilled on all sides.

5. Place the lettuce leaves in a bowl followed by the mayonnaise.

6. Place the grilled shrimp on top and serve.

16.Chicken Satay

On Monday nights, the gang opts for Thai food. Sheldon orders Chicken Satay with extra peanut sauce from a restaurant named Siam palace. You will love this delicious version of the dish.

Serving size: 4

Cooking time: 45 minutes

Ingredients:

- 1 tablespoon soy sauce
- 2 teaspoons Indian curry powder (Garam Masala)
- 1 teaspoon turmeric powder
- 1 tablespoon garlic, chopped
- 5 tablespoon coconut milk
- ½ inch ginger, chopped
- 2 teaspoons fish sauce
- 2 lb chicken, chopped
- 1 tablespoon vegetable oil
- Salt and pepper to taste

Instructions:

1. Add the coconut milk, curry powder, garlic, turmeric, ginger, fish sauce and soy sauce to a bowl and mix.

2. Toss in chicken pieces and rest for 3 hours or overnight.

3. Remove chicken from the marinade and poke them through a skewer.

4. Brush the oil on top and sprinkle with salt and pepper.

5. Heat grill to medium heat and place the chicken.

6. Turn them occasionally and cook for 20 minutes or until tender.

7. Serve hot.

17. Beef Brisket

Although never seen on the show, Howard's mom makes heavenly brisket. She serves them with potatoes and carrots, which he carries in a Tupperware box.

Serving size: 6

Cooking time: 8 hours

Ingredients:

- 4 lb beef, chopped
- 1 cup barbeque sauce
- 5 tablespoons soy sauce
- 1 cup water
- 2 potatoes, sliced
- 2 carrots, sliced

Instructions:

1. Add barbeque sauce, soy sauce and water to a bowl.

2. Place the beef brisket on a lined tray and pour the sauce mix all over.

3. Wrap foil all around the beef and make a couple of holes.

4. Place the potatoes and carrots around the beef.

5. Bake for 4 hours.

6. Slice the meat across the grain and serve hot with potatoes and carrots.

18. Mee Krob

Another one from Monday nights, Mee Krob is a Thai noodle dish that the gang loves to dig into. You will also fall in love with this dish!

Serving size: 8

Cooking time: 30 minutes

Ingredients:

- 1 tablespoon garlic, chopped
- 1 orange, sliced
- ¼ cup dried shrimp

- 2 teaspoons fish sauce
- 2 shallots, chopped
- 4 ounces tofu
- 8 tablespoons sugar
- 3 cups vermicelli noodles
- 1 tablespoon soy sauce

Instructions:

1. Add oil to a pan and toss in garlic, shallots and tofu and brown evenly.

2. Add in fish sauce, sugar and soy sauce.

3. Heat oil in a skillet and fry the noodles. They should puff up as soon as they hit the oil.

4. Fry the shrimp in the same oil for about 2 minutes.

5. Add the shrimp and noodles to the sauce and toss for a minute.

6. Serve hot.

19. Giacomo's Pizza!

Sheldon orders himself a pizza from Giacomo's topped with sausages, mushrooms and olives.

PS: If you are lactose intolerant like Leonard then you might want to skip the cheese!

Serving size: 4

Cooking time: 40 minutes

Ingredients:

- 1 tablespoon oil
- 4 ounces sausage

- 3 ounces mushrooms, chopped
- 1 tablespoon garlic, chopped
- 1 onion, sliced
- 2 tablespoons basil leaves, chopped
- 1 pack pizza crust
- ½ cup pizza sauce
- 2 cups mozzarella cheese, grated

Instructions:

1. Preheat oven to 400 Fahrenheit.

2. Add oil to a pan and toss in garlic and sausages and cook for 5 minutes.

3. Place the pizza crust on a plate and spread the tomato sauce evenly.

4. Add the pork, mushrooms sliced onion and basil leaves all over.

5. Sprinkle the cheese on top.

6. Bake for 25 to 30 minutes or until the cheese melts and the sausages are soft.

7. Serve hot.

20. Beef with Broccoli

Beef with Broccoli is a staple dish that Sheldon orders for the gang. He thinks the menu he orders is perfect for a gang of four boys.

Serving size: 4

Cooking time: 15 minutes

Ingredients:

- 2 tablespoons flour
- 1 lb steak
- 2 tablespoons brown sugar
- 1 tablespoon garlic, chopped
- ½ inch ginger, chopped
- 2 tablespoons oil
- 3 cups broccoli
- ½ cup onions, chopped

Instructions:

1. Add flour, and 2 tablespoons water to a bowl and toss in the beef.

2. To another bowl, add sugar, garlic, ginger and soy sauce and mix until well combined.

3. Heat a pan and add in oil and beef and cook until brown on all sides.

4. Toss in the broccoli and pour in the soy sauce mix.

5. Cook until tender and serve hot with noodles or rice.

21. Peach Cobbler Chicken

Sheldon's mom makes him a Peach Chicken Cobbler using lard. Here's a simple recipe to try out.

Serving size: 4

Cooking time: 45 minutes

Ingredients:

- 4 chicken breasts
- 2 tablespoons oil
- ¼ cup peaches, chopped
- 1 ¼ cup stock
- 1 tablespoon corn starch
- Salt and pepper to taste

Instructions:

1. Add oil to a pan and brown chicken on all sides.

2. Remove chicken and set aside.

3. Add stock to the pan and toss in the peaches.

4. Allow them to soften fully before adding the chicken and cook for 10 minutes.

5. Add in corn starch, salt and pepper.

6. Serve hot.

22. Cashew Chicken

Sheldon often orders Cashew Chicken from Schezuan Palace. Once it closes, Leonard stacks 4,000 takeout boxes from the restaurant and hides the fact from Sheldon. He orders the same dish from another restaurant named Golden Dragon, packs it in these boxes and gives it to Sheldon.

Serving size: 4

Cooking time: 30 minutes

Ingredients:

- 1 tablespoon flour
- 3 tablespoons soy sauce

- 3 tablespoons vinegar
- 2 teaspoons sesame oil
- Pepper to taste
- 1 lb chicken
- 2 tablespoons oil
- 1 tablespoon garlic, chopped
- 1 onion, chopped
- 1 bell pepper, chopped
- 5 tablespoons water
- ¼ cup roasted cashews, roughly chopped

Instructions:

1. Add flour, soy sauce, vinegar, sesame oil and pepper to a bowl and toss in the chicken.

2. Mix and rest for 10 minutes.

3. Add oil to a pan and toss in the garlic and onion.

4. Add the chicken and cook for 2 minutes.

5. Toss in the peppers and water and bring to a boil.

6. Mix in the cashews and cook for a minute.

7. Serve hot with fried rice.

23. Vegetable Lo Mein

When it comes to Chinese take outs, it's not just non-vegetarian foods that appeal to the gang, but also a few veg options like Vegetable Lo Mein. Here's a simple recipe for the same.

Serving size: 4

Cooking time: 20 minutes

Ingredients:

- 10 ounces Lo Mein noodles
- 2 teaspoons oil
- 1 bell pepper, chopped
- 1 carrot, chopped
- 1 cup peas
- 1 tablespoon garlic, chopped
- 2 tablespoons soy sauce
- 1 teaspoon sesame oil
- ½ teaspoon sugar
- Sesame seeds to sprinkle

Instructions:

1. Add noodles to boiling water and cook till soft.

2. Add oil to a pan and toss in the garlic, pepper, carrots and peas.

3. Add in sesame oil, soy sauce and sugar and mix.

4. Toss in the noodles and mix well.

5. Serve with a sprinkling of sesame on top.

24. Shrimp in Mobster sauce

Yep, you read that right, it was an intentional typo. When the gang visits a Chinese restaurant, Sheldon finds "Shrimp in Mobster Sauce" on the menu, which makes him assume that the restaurant engages in criminal activities. You don't have to worry about any such thing. You only have to try out this delicious shrimp in lobster sauce recipe.

Serving size: 2

Cooking time: 20 minutes

Ingredients:

- 10 ounces shrimp
- 4 ounces pork, minced
- 3 tablespoons vegetable oil
- 1 teaspoon sesame oil
- 1 teaspoon garlic, minced
- 2 tablespoons wine
- 1 cup chicken broth
- 1 teaspoon sugar
- 1 cup peas
- 1 egg
- 5 whole spring onions, chopped
- Salt and pepper to taste

Instructions:

1. Add pork to boiling water and cook till soft.

2. Add oil to a pan along with the garlic, cooked pork, peas and shrimp and toss for a minute.

3. Add vinegar, broth, salt, pepper, sesame oil and sugar and cook for 2 minutes.

4. Beat the eggs and spring onions together and pour over the pork mixture and cook for a minute or two.

5. Serve hot.

25. General Tso's Chicken

As we know, Sheldon is very particular about his meal choices as also menu cards. On one particular occasion, he is displeased that General Tso's Chicken is mentioned in the "chicken" section and not the "specials" section.

Serving size: 4

Cooking time: 30 minutes

Ingredients:

- 1 lb chicken, skinless
- 2 teaspoons garlic, chopped

- ½ inch ginger, minced
- 1 teaspoon chili flakes
- 5 tablespoons corn starch
- Oil for frying

For sauce

- 1 teaspoon Hoisin sauce
- 2 tablespoons rice vinegar
- 4 tablespoons soy sauce
- 5 tablespoons water
- 2 tablespoons corn starch
- 2 tablespoons sugar

Instructions:

1. Cut the chicken into small pieces and add to a bowl along with the corn starch.

2. Mix and rest for an hour.

3. Add hoisin sauce, vinegar, soy sauce, water and sugar to a bowl and mix well.

4. Add oil to a pan and fry the chicken until golden and crispy.

5. Pat them dry and sprinkle chili flakes all over.

6. Add a teaspoon oil to a pan and sauté the garlic.

7. Pour in the sauce mixture and the chicken and toss.

8. Cook for a minute.

9. Serve hot.

Chapter 3: Desserts

26. Raj's Tapioca Pudding

Raj's love for Tapioca pudding knows no bounds albeit, Sheldon doesn't share the same sentiment! He thinks chocolate puddings are better. Why don't you try out this recipe and decide for yourself?

Serving size: 4

Cooking time: 30 minutes

Ingredients:

- 1/2 cup tapioca pearls (sago)
- 5 cups milk
- 1 cup sugar
- 2 teaspoons vanilla extract
- 1 teaspoon corn starch

Instructions:

1. Add milk to a sauce pan along with the sugar and bring to a boil.

2. Add in the tapioca and simmer for 40 minutes or until the tapioca is soft.

3. Add in the vanilla extract and mix.

4. Mix in corn starch to thicken the mixture.

5. Serve hot.

27. Sheldon's Birthday Cake

Sheldon tells Bernadette that he loves chocolate cake with strawberry frosting. He also tells her that he doesn't like birthday text mentioned in caps as though the cake is yelling at him.

Serving size: 6

Cooking time: 1 hour

Ingredients:

For cake

- ½ cup butter, melted
- 1 cup buttermilk
- 1 teaspoon vanilla
- 2 cups sugar
- 1 teaspoon baking powder
- 1 cup black coffee, hot
- 1 cup cocoa powder, unsweetened
- 2 cups flour

For frosting

- 1 cup butter, melted
- 5 tablespoons strawberry jam
- 3 cups sugar
- 2 tablespoons cream

Instructions:

1. Add flour, sugar, baking powder, cocoa powder to a bowl and mix.

2. Beat the eggs along with the buttermilk, butter and vanilla.

3. Combine the two and pour in hot coffee.

4. Fold the mixture. Don't worry if the batter is thin.

5. Pour into a lined baking dish.

6. Bake in a preheated 375 Fahrenheit oven for 40 minutes.

7. To make the frosting, beat sugar and butter until creamy.

8. Mix in the jam and sugar and beat until light and fluffy.

9. Allow cake to cool for an hour before cutting it in half.

10. Spread 4 tablespoons of the frosting between the layers.

11. Apply the rest over the cake and serve.

28. Nutty Muffins

Who doesn't love muffins? Sheldon and Leonard are often seen biting into delicious muffins! Here is a simple recipe for you to try out. Enjoy!

Serving size: 6-8

Cooking time: 30 minutes

Ingredients:

- 2 tablespoons butter, melted
- ½ cup milk
- 2 eggs

- 3 cups sugar
- 4 cups flour
- 1 teaspoon baking powder
- 1 cup dry fruits (cashews, almonds, raisins)
- ½ cup chocolate chips

Instructions:

1. Preheat the oven to 400 Fahrenheit.

2. Add the eggs to a bowl and beat for a minute or until fluffy.

3. Add the melted butter, milk, sugar and mix until combined.

4. Add the flour and baking powder and fold the mixture.

5. Fold in the nuts and chocolate chips and pour a tablespoon of the mixture in lined cupcake tins.

6. Bake for 15 minutes or until they are ready.

7. Serve warm.

29. Memaw's Christmas Cookies

Sheldon loves the simple yet delicious Christmas cookies that his mom bakes. Amy calls her up for the recipe and bakes him a batch for Christmas. He falls in love with them and tells her the cookies taste like his mom's hugs.

Serving size: 10-12

Cooking time: 30 minutes

Ingredients:

- 2 cups butter
- 1 cup sugar
- 1 large egg
- 3 ¼ cup flour
- 1 teaspoon Almond extract
- Sugar sprinkles

Instructions:

1. Preheat oven to 380 Fahrenheit.

2. Add sugar, butter and almond extract to a bowl and beat till fluffy.

3. Tip in the flour and fold the mixture.

4. Knead into a dough and roll it out to ½ inch thickness.

5. Use cookie cutters of your choice and place them on a baking tray.

6. Bake for 12 minutes and serve with sugar sprinkles on top.

30. Ice Cream with Kalua

Penny loves ice creams and often turns to them to fix a bad mood. She and Amy enjoy coffee liqueur with their ice cream. Here's a recipe for Kaluha ice cream, which takes the taste game up a notch.

Serving size: 20

Cooking time: 30 minutes (5 hours freeze time)

Ingredients:

- 2 cups milk
- 2 cups cream

- 1 cup sugar
- 2 tablespoons instant coffee powder
- 5 tablespoons Kaluha liqueur
- 6 eggs

Instructions:

1. Add the milk, liqueur, sugar, coffee powder and cream to a pan and bring to a boil.

2. Separate the eggs and add the yolks to a bowl.

3. Beat them until they are stiff.

4. Pour a ladleful of the hot milk mixture into the yolks and beat fast. Make sure the yolks do not scramble.

5. Slowly pour the egg mixture into the remaining milk mixture and stir for 3 to 4 minutes or until thick.

6. Pour the mixture through a sieve and cover with cling film.

7. Refrigerate the mixture for 5 hours and serve.

Conclusion

And there you have it. 30 delicious recipes to throw the ultimate Big Bang Theory party. Don't forget to try each one of them and catch fans by surprise.

Feel free to switch up the ingredients and give the recipes a spin. Well, it's time to hit the kitchen and reach for the ingredients.

Enjoy, enjoy, enjoy.

Made in the USA
Las Vegas, NV
19 November 2024

12103557R00046